365 DAYS OF

kindness

DAILY GUIDANCE FOR
HAPPINESS AND GRATITUDE

summersdale

365 DAYS OF KINDNESS

An Hachette UK Company
www.hachette.co.uk

Summersdale Publishers Ltd
Part of Octopus Publishing Group Limited
Carmelite House
50 Victoria Embankment
LONDON
EC4Y 0DZ
UK

www.summersdale.com

Printed and bound in China

ISBN: 978-1-80007-100-1

Substantial discounts on bulk quantities of Summersdale books are available to corporations, professional associations and other organizations. For details contact general enquiries: telephone: +44 (0) 1243 771107 or email: enquiries@summersdale.com.

To ....

From ....

introduction

An act of kindness can transform someone's day, and its effects may be even more far-reaching — cheering them up when they're at a low point in their life or inspiring them to pay your act of generosity forward. The good news gets even better: carrying out compassionate acts will benefit *you* as much as the recipient. Acts of kindness give you a sense of purpose and belonging, and also release feel-good chemicals in the brain, triggering a warm glow of contentment.

Being kind doesn't necessarily mean carrying out grand gestures or spending large amounts of money. This book includes plenty of ideas for simple kindnesses and ways to spread positivity, along with inspirational quotes to remind you of the benefits of benevolence. There are a few suggestions for helping your local wildlife, and supporting the environment, too.

Kindness and gratitude go hand in hand, so we'll look at ways to recognize and appreciate the blessings we receive as well. By practising gratitude you'll get a better perspective on your day. Self-compassion is another important skill that can affect your well-being on every level; there are ideas to help you develop this in the pages that follow.

So, welcome to your year of compassion! Enjoy working through the tips — adapting them or picking and choosing those that appeal to you — but most of all, enjoy experiencing 365 days of kindness.

january

Start with a smile. Smiling is a simple act of kindness, but it's a powerful one as it spreads happiness and will boost your mood, too. Begin the day by smiling at yourself in the mirror and then challenge yourself to smile at someone else — friend, family or stranger. You'll soon feel full of positivity and ready to start your kindness mission!

Phone an older relative or neighbour, or — even better — pop in to catch up in person. Conversation and contact with others are so important for our mental health, and a good chat is the perfect way to keep the January blues at bay.

Love and kindness
go hand in hand.

MARIAN KEYES

Start a kindness journal — a record of the
compassionate acts that others have done for you,
along with notes of kindnesses you've read about
and ideas for things you can do for others. You
could treat yourself to a special notebook or do this
on your phone. Your journal will be a great source
of inspiration and a mood-boosting read before
you go to sleep at night.

A feel-good movie will remind you of the power of kindness and inspire you to take action, so settle down to watch one today. *Wonder, A Beautiful Day in the Neighborhood* or *Pay it Forward* are all good choices.

Be inclusive and make a move to welcome those who are new — or feel out of place — in a social situation. Even a small gesture, such as being the first person to speak to them or show them around, can make a big difference.

•••（07）•••

Write to someone who inspires you and tell them why — you'll make their day.

··●(08)●··

Plant up a pot of bulbs and give to a friend or neighbour to brighten up their home on gloomy winter days. They'll appreciate the trouble you've gone to and will remember your kindness whenever they catch sight of your flowers.

··●(09)●··

Pause and acknowledge the importance of being kind to *yourself*. The way you treat yourself will affect the way others treat you. Learning to see yourself in a positive light and to nurture and care for yourself will genuinely change your life, so make a commitment to be kind to yourself every day from now on.

Give someone a cosy gift. A pair of woolly socks, a warm hat, a pack of hot chocolate or a scented candle will bring some warmth to chilly evenings.

Make a note of something you're grateful for every day. You'll find yourself looking out for these blessings as they happen.

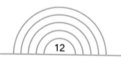

Just imagine how different the world could be if we all spoke to everyone with kindness and respect.

HOLLY BRANSON

Being a considerate driver is a great way of extending kindness to strangers, and of making the roads a safer place to be. You'll improve the mood of your fellow road-users, which will mean that they're far more likely to extend similar patience to others, too. If you don't drive, you can still be civil to others when commuting or even walking through town.

Always... try to be a little kinder than is necessary.

J. M. BARRIE

Choose your words kindly. Spend a moment thinking about how impactful the things you say can be. Words are powerful: they represent what you're thinking and who you are, and they live on in other people's memories. So stop and think carefully before you speak — and spread kindness whenever you can.

Extend the power of positive words to your self-talk. Many of us judge ourselves harshly, so pause when you notice you're thinking unkind thoughts about your own achievements and abilities. Reframe these thoughts in a kind way — you'll feel happier, and your loved ones will enjoy your new-found positivity, too.

••• (17) •••

This year, you're going to remember your friends' and family's birthdays — so get organized! Put them all in the calendar, setting a reminder if you want to send a card or a celebratory text. If you plan ahead, you can handmake cards or create a photo card online to make them smile.

••• (18) •••

Paying a compliment is a wonderful way of spreading warmth and happiness: it can make someone's day, or have an even more powerful impact, making the recipient feel valued and changing the way they feel about themselves. Be specific and sincere, and your compliments will go a long way.

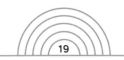

True beauty is born through our actions and aspirations and in the kindness we offer to others.

ALEK WEK

Try a loving-kindness meditation. Sit comfortably in a quiet space. Focus on your breathing: breathe in peace and breathe out tension. When you feel calm and grounded, imagine unconditional love emanating from your heart and filling your body. Enjoy the sensation of acceptance and contentment, letting stray thoughts come and go and refocusing when you need to. Finish your meditation with three deep breaths. With practice you'll be able to tap into these feelings throughout your day.

••• (21) •••

Sometimes the gift of time out can be the best gift of all. Give a loved one some well-earned time off by walking their dog or babysitting so that they can take a few hours to relax.

••• (22) •••

Make a donation to a charity that means a lot to you. It will support their valuable work and give you a boost, too. It could be a one-off gift or a small regular payment — whatever you can manage.

••• (23) •••

If you don't have spare funds to donate, you can still support a charity by spreading the word about their campaigns on social media and signing relevant petitions.

Choose a book for a friend or loved one, or pass on something you've read and know they will enjoy. It's a lovely way to show them that they're in your thoughts. You could include a (handmade) bookmark, or a note tucked in the pages explaining why you think they'll enjoy it.

If the only prayer you said in your whole life was "thank you", that would suffice.

MEISTER ECKHART

••• •••

One of the most powerful kindnesses we can practise is acceptance. Everyone has their faults, their quirks and their weaknesses — and most of the time they're doing the very best they can to cope with life's ups and downs. Rather than picking up on your family's or colleagues' "negative" traits, focus on their positive qualities.

••• (27) •••

Self-acceptance is just as important, so spend a little time thinking about how your "flaws" are not imperfections; they're part of what makes you unique. Make a list of your positive traits — ask a close friend or family member to help you if you're stuck — and celebrate your achievements instead.

28

Be kinder to yourself. And then let
your kindness flood the world.

PEMA CHODRON

Customize some compassionate acts today.
Make a list of five people you know who really
need cheering up or deserve a treat, and choose
something appropriate that you can do for them.
(Remember, you don't need to buy expensive gifts
— a thoughtful act that shows you care will be just
as meaningful.)

Chore challenge — see if you can carry out a task for a co-worker or housemate anonymously, so that they come into the workplace or return home and find it already done for them.

Have a kindness review. Take a look back at your journal for the past month and celebrate all you've achieved. Are there any acts of kindness you'd like to repeat or improve on? Jot down any ideas for new things you could try out next month.

february

With the first signs of spring in the air, think about the positives of spring cleaning and bringing new energy to a space. You could declutter a communal area at work or in the home to freshen things up and cheer up your colleagues or housemates.

Search online for stories of how acts of kindness have benefitted other people's lives for the better. These accounts are a brilliant source of inspiration and heart-warming, too. The site www.randomactsofkindness.org is a good starting point, or search for "random acts of kindness" on your favourite social media platform.

Take some well-earned time out and wind down by learning a new craft. Studies have shown that focusing on crafting benefits our mental health, giving our mind and body a chance to relax. Maybe you could share your skills once you've had a little practice, or even create some gifts for loved ones.

Be kind to bees! The planet's top pollinators play a key part in the production of around a third of everything we eat, but they're in serious decline. They are in dire need of kindness — plant bee-friendly flowers if you have space, or campaign to help save them and spread the word.

You'll be doing yourself a great kindness if you spend 15 minutes outside connecting with nature once a day. This will benefit your physical and mental well-being and will leave you feeling calmer, which makes it much easier to be a kind and considerate person!

••• 06 •••

Put yourself in someone else's shoes. This is a good practice when it comes to keeping the peace and understanding other people's points of view. While you're thinking through someone else's situation, see if you can come up with something that you could do to help them, or a gesture they might appreciate.

••• (07) •••

Music is a great mood booster, so make a playlist of meaningful songs for someone you care about... or just dedicate a single track to them and send them the link.

••• (08) •••

Pay for someone behind you in the queue. You could treat them to their morning coffee or their groceries, or visit a book shop and surprise the next book lover standing in line.

••• (09) •••

Reply to a post you enjoy on social media. It's easy to swipe past in the blink of an eye, but taking the time to leave a supportive comment helps to make the internet a positive place.

Feeling gratitude and not expressing it is like wrapping a present and not giving it.

WILLIAM ARTHUR WARD

••• (11) •••

If you have been practising your loving-kindness meditation (see 20 January, page 14) you can extend this by sending compassionate thoughts to others. Practise the meditation as described, then picture yourself beaming loving kindness out to those around you. Begin with those who are closest to you — your family and close friends — then extend this further to other friends and acquaintances. You may finish your meditation by picturing your love extending to people around the globe. This is a wonderful practice to try every evening before you sleep.

Today, think about who would benefit from some words of encouragement. Give their confidence a boost by telling them that you believe in them. Many of us struggle with self-doubt — especially if we're facing a challenging situation — but hearing someone else say "You can do it" can be the very thing we need to help us succeed.

Be kind to the planet and our resources by only using what you need and reusing items if possible. Remind yourself of the recycling guidelines in your area and recycle any waste that you can. There may be other recycling facilities in your area — for batteries, ink cartridges and electrical goods — so check these out, too.

••• (14) •••

Meditate on love and what it means to you. Think about everyone who is special to you and consider why they mean so much. What are their positive qualities? You'll remind yourself of how blessed you are to have these precious people in your life.

••• (15) •••

Look for opportunities to be helpful to others — whether it's holding open a door, helping someone who's struggling to lift their baby's buggy onto a bus, or passing them something out of reach in the supermarket. Your thoughtfulness and consideration will be just as well received as the act itself.

Write a cheerful note for your partner/child/housemate and hide it in their bag to make them smile when they find it later in the day.

••• (17) •••

Happy "Random Acts of Kindness Day"! Look out online today for posts about this celebration of the power of small selfless gestures — share them and jot down ideas for anything you could try yourself.

••• (18) •••

Preparing food for someone is a lovely gesture, and it's one that you can adapt to your skills and budget, too. Whether you surprise your housemate with a three-course meal or bake a cake for a neighbour, it's the thought that counts.

If you know someone who's going through a tricky time, make them a happiness jar. Write inspirational quotes, affirmations and compliments on slips of paper and put them in a jar, so they can pick one out at random whenever they need cheering up.

••• 20 •••

Develop a positive outlook. It will enable you to be kinder to others — and to yourself. And did you know that positive people enjoy better mental and physical health and tend to achieve more? It can take a little time, but practise looking on the bright side when things go wrong, and you can learn this skill just like any other.

No act of kindness, however small, is ever wasted.

AESOP

Can you think of someone who always goes that extra mile to provide excellent service, or who's always cheerful and kind while doing their job? Today, take the trouble to write to them or their employer and say how much you appreciate their efforts. Your praise will be a great reward for their hard work.

Keep a spare umbrella in your car or at work so that you can lend it to someone caught out by the rain. (A spare pen, tissues and some basic first-aid supplies are handy items to have to help others, too.)

Be kind to yourself and do something that you want to do, rather than something that you *need* to do. If you can, find space for a ten-minute moment like this every day — to have some hobby time, read, play with your pet, or just relax.

● ● ● ● ● ●

Try to learn a few words or phrases in a co-worker or friend's first language and practise them with your pal. Your pronunciation may not be perfect, but they will be moved by your efforts and thoughtfulness.

● ● ● (26) ● ● ●

Learning to say "I'm sorry" can be a challenge, but apologizing when you're in the wrong is a gracious thing to do. If you owe anyone an apology, swallow your pride and say sorry sincerely. You'll both feel better for it.

● ● ● (27) ● ● ●

Compliment a parent on the way their child is behaving. You will make their day.

Leave a note in a library book for the next borrower to find. You could say what you've enjoyed about it (no spoilers!), wish them a happy reading journey, or just leave them a smiley face and a "hello". If it's a book with a twist at the end, you could add something amusing after the last page: "I didn't see that coming," for example!

••• 29 •••

Reconnect with an old friend. Life rushes by so quickly that it's easy for us to lose touch. Find 15 minutes to sit down and send a message to rebuild a connection — you won't regret it!

march

Think about the kindest person you know and take your inspiration from them. There's sure to be something you can learn — what kindnesses have they shown to you and others? Can you carry out similar acts or cultivate their qualities?

Volunteer to help a local cause — there will be so many opportunities to do this in your community. Whatever your skillset, there's sure to be some way you can help someone else. Volunteering improves your mental health, gives you a sense of worth and perspective, and — of course — benefits others, so research some local options and take the first step today.

Practise gratitude at work by thanking your colleagues for anything they've done to help you. Take a moment to think about whether your workplace is somewhere that acknowledges everyone's efforts and makes employees feel valued. If that's not the case, is there anything you can do to make people's work lives more positive? Can you start a gratitude board, where people pin up names of co-workers who've gone the extra mile and helped them? Or could you suggest a monthly email recognizing everyone's achievements?

●●● **04** ●●●

Build a birdhouse to give your garden visitors a place to set up home.

••● 05 ●••

If you have some free time, could you volunteer at your local community centre to help make the teas and coffees for the groups that meet there? You will meet new people and help to create a welcoming space for group members.

••● 06 ●••

Try out a new local retailer. It's a kindness to your community (and the environment) to shop locally when you can and support the small businesses near you.

••● 07 ●••

Kindness often involves putting the needs of others before ourselves, so look for the opportunity to do that today. You could give up your break to lend a sympathetic ear to a friend, for example.

Be kind to yourself by making sure that you get enough good quality sleep. Get an early night, try out a kindness meditation as you drop off and you'll feel much better for it in the morning.

Just be kind. The act itself is free, and it's priceless.

LADY GAGA

••• (10) •••

Wait until the temperature has reached 10°C (50°F) before doing a spring tidy up of your garden. This will give all those beneficial insects who are hibernating in plant stalks and fallen leaves the chance to wake up.

Spend a moment thinking through an act of kindness or a favour that someone else has carried out for you. Consider in depth the trouble that went into the gesture. We can often take other people's kindnesses for granted or dash off a quick thank-you without really appreciating what they have done for us. Once you've truly acknowledged their efforts to yourself, send them a sincere thank-you note.

What you do makes a difference and you have to decide what kind of a difference you want to make.

JANE GOODALL

Why not take an interest in a friend's hobby by researching it or asking them to demonstrate it to you? Your friend will love sharing their passion, and you'll spend some quality time together, too.

••• (14) •••

Take a photo of something beautiful in your local environment and share it on social media to brighten everyone's day: a spectacular cloud formation; a close-up of a flower; or a detail of an unusual building.

••• (15) •••

You're amazing — let this be your mantra for the day. Say it to yourself in the mirror and then go out and tell someone else they're amazing, too.

Give some thought to how you could bring a more neighbourly feel to your street or apartment block. Could you organize a clean-up, get together with your neighbours to produce some street art, or have a street-meet once a week, where everyone takes a coffee or glass of wine outside and catches up?

••• (17) •••

You've already tried putting yourself in someone else's shoes, so now try to walk in them. Imagining how someone is feeling is a great start, but take your empathy further by asking others about their lives and opinions, visiting a different place of worship or volunteering in a different community.

Give birds a helping hand with their springtime nest-building by leaving out natural fibres and pruned plant materials in a hanging basket or bush near to where they may want to nest. Cut lengths of natural twine or wool down to less than 15 cm (6 in.). Don't put out human hair, which can entangle birds, and only put out pet hair if your pet hasn't received any anti-parasite treatment.

Too often we underestimate the power of a touch, a smile, a kind word, a listening ear...

LEO BUSCAGLIA

A simple way to be kind to nature is to take a bin bag whenever you visit a natural beauty spot and collect any litter you find along the way. Sadly, it's all too easy to fill a bag with food wrappers, discarded coffee cups, and so on, but it's very satisfying to know that you've made a difference with such a simple activity.

If your local school has a visiting book fair or sends round book-sale fliers for children, donate a small amount to your child's class — or to the school in general — for those children who can't afford to buy a new book.

••• (22) •••

Treat your pet to a little more of your attention, an extra walk, or their favourite thing to eat. (If you don't have a pet, treat someone else's!)

••• (23) •••

If someone you know is struggling to finish a project, help out. Perhaps you can give them some advice or a different perspective or take on some of their other responsibilities to give them time to focus on the task in hand.

••• (24) •••

Transform your conversations by seeing them as an opportunity to learn, rather than to speak – this will benefit you as an exercise in mindfulness, too. Keep this in mind when you listen to others today.

The gifts of caring, attention, affection, appreciation, and love are some of the most precious gifts you can give.

DEEPAK CHOPRA

Reach out to an elderly person in your community who lives alone. Research in the US and the UK shows that around 45 per cent of seniors experience loneliness. Perhaps you can plan a regular visit to a neighbour or befriend someone through a charity such as Age UK or Friend to Friend America, or volunteer with your local library to drop books off for someone who can't get out and about.

●●● (27) ●●●

Be kind to your future self! Draw up a list of treats to save up for and then look forward to your reward or plan your schedule so that you can take some time off and relax.

●●● (28) ●●●

Strong connections are essential when promoting kindness, so think about those you have and consider ways you could improve them. Do you need to devote more time to a friend or clear the air after a misunderstanding, for example?

●●● (29) ●●●

Spread positivity by being the person who turns negative conversations around today. If someone is stuck in a loop of complaining about the same old thing, see if you can divert the conversation down a cheerier route, or even solve the problem!

Deliberately seek opportunities for kindness, sympathy, and patience.

EVELYN UNDERHILL

Have a kindness check-in today and focus on how you feel after carrying out small daily acts of kindness. Notice feelings of warmth, connection, happiness. Have you seen any changes in your nearest and dearest, too? Kindness begets kindness, so the effects of your new regime may be spreading — make a few notes in your journal or on your phone, and check back on your progress again in a month or so.

april

Make someone laugh! The gift of laughter is a great kindness, so learn a few jokes to share: What do you call a line of rabbits hopping backward? ... A receding hare line! ... See!

Get together with neighbours to plant up a communal flowerbed, vegetable plot or even some pretty containers. You'll all enjoy a greater sense of community, working together on your project, and your neighbourhood will benefit from the flowers or veggies, too.

03

The best way to find yourself is to lose yourself in the service of others.

MAHATMA GANDHI

••• **04** •••

Make a gratitude collage with photos of all the things you appreciate. Include happy moments, friends and achievements. Display your collage where you'll catch sight of it every day.

••• **05** •••

Actively look for the good in others. Everyone has their good qualities, so focus on these and appreciate them with every interaction.

Become an ally to people with a disability in your community and lift their voices. The best way to do this — and to educate yourself about issues of accessibility, language and inclusivity — is to read (and share) some of the brilliant blogs out there.

Say "hello" to a stranger — and follow it up with a comment about the weather, your surroundings or a compliment if you can. The connections we make with others — even brief ones — can bring so much positivity to our day. You may hear an inspirational story from your new acquaintance, or even make a new friend — and you'll certainly brighten their day.

Public service is about serving all the people, including the ones who are not like you.

CONSTANCE WU

Compile a directory for your street, including your neighbours' names, what their pets are called, a fascinating fact about themselves and a note of any skills they're willing to share. Give everyone a copy — it's a nice introduction for anyone new moving into your road, too.

••• 10 •••

Make your choices eco-friendly. You could buy sustainable cotton, or choose bamboo items rather than plastic ones.

••• (11) •••

Challenge yourself to find out something new about a co-worker or acquaintance. Taking the time to get to know someone a little better will add a spark of happiness to their day — and yours — as you make a new connection.

••• (12) •••

Spread some happiness by sharing any positive news stories you come across on social media.

••• (13) •••

Bring awareness to your thoughts. Notice when you find yourself judging someone by their appearance. Remind yourself that there is more to everyone than meets the eye.

When given the choice between being right or being kind, choose kind.

WAYNE W. DYER

Harness your superpower! We all have a special skill or talent; whether it's art, photography, DIY... or something less practical but just as valuable, such as the gift of encouraging others to do their best. Spend a little time today thinking about how you can use your ability to benefit others — starting a photography club at a school, or doing odd jobs for neighbours, for example — and then put your plan into action!

Learn from the southern African tradition of *ubuntu* — the idea that one person cannot be happy unless the people around them are happy, too. It's a philosophy that encourages us to share our resources and take responsibility as a community to look after one another.

•••(17)•••

When you're doing your weekly shop, look out for brands that will donate to charity when you purchase them or give something back to the environment.

•••(18)•••

Make an effort to brighten up your yard or the front of your home — plant some sunflowers or add a decoration that passers-by can appreciate and enjoy.

Acting as a mentor to someone can be a very fulfilling role, where you put your experience to good use and benefit someone starting out in an area you're familiar with. Consider whether you could do this – either at work, college or in a less formal way. A good mentor gets to know their "mentee" and offers advice in a way that works best for them. You will learn just as much about yourself, too.

Could you save a little money this month by forgoing coffees or other treats to fund an act of kindness? You may have a specific beneficiary in mind, or look for someone deserving while you save. Enjoy watching your fund – and anticipation – build up.

Go through your wardrobe and pick out any items you no longer wear and donate them to charity.

••• 22 •••

Who can you read a story to? Reading aloud is a heart-warming activity to share with someone — it doesn't have to be a child! If you live alone, would your local care home or school like you to go in and spend some time reading there?

••• 23 •••

Show your appreciation for your local emergency service unit. Write a letter or send a card thanking the personnel for all they do.

Make a "hug in a box" and send it to someone who needs comforting. You could include chocolates, pamper products, a book, tea or coffee, cookies, candles, puzzle books or a card game.

••• 25 •••

Try to remember the details of conversations with people you bump into, so that you can ask them how things are going next time you meet. If you make a point of remembering someone's latest project, or asking after their children by name, they'll appreciate it.

••• 26 •••

Compassion is contagious. Every moment we choose compassion, we move toward a better world.

AMIT RAY

The best way to be kind to the environment is to reduce your carbon footprint, so do some research about what you can do to improve yours. Can you use less energy in your home or eat less meat, for example? Take a look at www.climatecare.org for tips.

Practise paying it forward — the idea is to do a good deed for someone once you've received a good deed yourself, and encourage them to pass on a similar kindness, spreading happiness and compassion. You can even download Pay it Forward cards to explain what you're doing.

••• (29) •••

Carry out an act of kindness at the supermarket and take back someone else's trolley when you return your own.

••• (30) •••

A great way to be kind to nature is to set up a local project to support wildlife. You could plant trees in a communal space, reclaim a parking space to set up a "parklet" — a mini park (contact your local authority for details of this simple process) — or create a bee street (get everyone to plant native flowers to provide a route for pollinators).

may

01

Give someone a hand-picked spray of flowers from your garden — or pick them responsibly in the countryside. (You shouldn't pick from parks, nature reserves or areas where flowers have been planted for decoration; and you should only take one out of every 20 wild blooms for your bunch.) Tie your mini bouquet with a ribbon and treat your lucky recipient to a burst of spring beauty.

02

Organize a fundraiser for your favourite charity or local cause, whether that's a coffee morning with some home bakes, a bring-and-buy sale, a raffle or charity car wash.

••• 03 •••

If someone you know is worried or anxious, give them the chance to talk about it. A sympathetic listener may be just what they need to feel that they're not alone. Doing an activity together — such as walking somewhere or grabbing a quick coffee — can create a great chance to chat without it feeling too intense. Give them your full attention and only offer advice if they ask for it.

••• 04 •••

Find out the name of someone you see regularly — such as your postal delivery person, the cashier in your local shop or your bus driver — and use it when you see them and say good morning.

Hold the door open for someone — it's a simple act, but it shows consideration, and you'll get the chance to smile at them, too. Two acts of kindness for the price of one!

••• (06) •••

Buy an extra can of food next time you do your weekly shop and donate it to your local foodbank.

••• (07) •••

Find a visual reminder to help you practise gratitude every day — it may be a photo you keep by your bedside or an inspiring quote on your kitchen noticeboard. When you see it, pause and think about everything you're grateful for in that moment.

As part of your quest to be kinder to the environment, take inspiration from the Māori tradition of *kaitiaki,* which means guarding the sea, sky and land. How could you protect and respect your environment? Is there a local beauty spot or natural feature that you could step forward to protect?

Think about how sincere you are when you ask people how they are, thank them or wish them a good day. Exchanging small talk is a great opportunity to show real warmth and interest in the people you meet every day, so bring sincerity to your interactions.

If you see someone without a smile, give them one of yours.

DOLLY PARTON

Combine fitness with fundraising and challenge yourself to train for a charity run, walk or swim. You could use an app to help you train for your goal.

•••（12）•••

Do something kind for a neighbour, whether that's taking in deliveries, sharing surplus food or even washing their car when you're doing your own.

Ask yourself: Have you been kind today? Make kindness your daily modus operandi and change your world.

ANNIE LENNOX

Next time your employer puts on a team-building day, suggest that you all work together to give something back to the community. A low-budget option is to do a beach clean together followed by a celebratory drink or two. If your company has a bigger budget to spend, consider projects such as refurbishing an area of a hospice, school or youth centre, or planning a marketing campaign for a charity. There are organizations who will help set up something suitable for you, along with more inspiration online.

••• (15) •••

Write a kind affirmation for yourself — such as "I am beautiful", "I am strong" or "I know I can do it" — and say it to yourself in the mirror this morning. Repeat often!

••• (16) •••

Offer to take a photo of a couple or family when you're out and about — your photo could well become a treasured possession, a special memory of their day together.

••• (17) •••

Support a local business by posting a picture online of something brilliant or delicious you've bought there. Search for the business on social media and tag them, too.

••• •••

Do something in memory of someone special who has passed away. You could take part in a sponsored walk or run; go on a "pilgrimage" to somewhere associated with them; gather memories in a book to share or plant a tree in remembrance of their life.

••• •••

Make a vow to become a more grateful or compassionate person — research shows that making a commitment in this way will lead to better results. You could make your oath more specific if you like: "I will be kinder to X at work", for example! Write down and recite your pledge.

Create a compost heap. You'll benefit the planet by recycling your fruit and vegetable peelings and garden clippings — rather than sending them to landfill — and by providing nutrients for micro-creatures and mini-beasts.

Next time you purchase a coffee, ask to pay for two, so that the café can pass a drink gifted by you on to someone less fortunate to enjoy.

A single act of kindness throws out roots in all directions.

AMELIA EARHART

Today practise being a good listener. This means focusing on the other person, thinking about what they're saying — and not jumping in and talking over them about your own experiences! They'll feel valued thanks to your improved listening skills, and you'll find that all your interactions improve if you practise regularly.

Cancel out bias: acknowledging that we are all biased to some degree — and then doing something about it — can help us to empathize and take a more balanced approach to others. Project Implicit offers online quizzes to help you identify unconscious bias, so think about completing one of these today.

It's important to support well-known charities and causes, but today find out about one of the hundreds of lesser-known charities out there and see if you can help them in any way. There may be a particular issue that resonates with you. (Check out www.smallcharities.org.uk or www.charitynavigator.org for ideas.)

Carry out a random act of kindness, with no expectation of reward, safe in the knowledge that one day someone might do the same for you.

DIANA, PRINCESS OF WALES

••• (27) •••

Donate unwanted blankets or towels to an animal shelter near you. They may also need old newspapers or pet food, so see if you can gather together a package of items.

••• (28) •••

Next time you're out and about, send someone a postcard. You don't need to go on holiday to do this — in fact, a postcard from your home town can be just as much fun.

••• (29) •••

Leave a thank-you for whoever delivers your mail. You could simply put up a note on your front door or mailbox, write them a rhyme, or leave them a card or cake.

Kind words produce their own image in men's souls, and a beautiful image it is.

BLAISE PASCAL

Practise sending thoughts of healing to someone who needs them. You could light a candle and do this in the form of a meditation if you like. Find a quiet moment, put your everyday thoughts aside and focus on sending them positive, loving energy.

june

Setting up a community group on social media for your village or local area can be really rewarding. Try to make it a positive place and start by posting inspiring pictures, information about facilities or notes about local history or legends. Invite people to share stories, knowledge, offers of help and support... As your group grows you may come up with plans for projects to improve your patch, too.

Think about how you could invest in your future development and what you need to progress. Make a plan to move forward, even if it's just by one small step at first.

Avoid spreading — or listening to — gossip. Gossip brings negative energy into your day and can, of course, be very hurtful. Share positive words instead.

Visit the Hunger Site, and click on the "Click to give" button. The site's sponsors will donate to a charity that delivers food to alleviate hunger around the world. It's a great cause, and an easy — and free — way to help people in need.

••• 05 •••

Be silly. Be kind. Be weird.
There's no time for anything else.

RICHARD GERE

••• 06 •••

If you can find common ground with someone
it's much easier to have a compassionate attitude,
so practise this today. Take a moment to think
about the similarities between yourself and the
people you meet, see on the news or read about
on social media. This is a good exercise to try
whenever you can; when you meet new people,
establishing these commonalities will help you to
build a good relationship.

How could you help your local hospital? The children's department may need toys, the neonatal unit might appreciate your knitting skills, or there may be a volunteer-run coffee shop that would welcome your help.

•••(08)•••

Spending time with pets gives us a brilliant well-being boost. If you have an animal companion, share the love with a friend who doesn't and invite them to walk the dog with you, for example.

•••(09)•••

A photo collage (or edit) is a thoughtful gift for a friend. Gather together a few favourite pictures and surprise someone with your creation.

It can be hard to be kind to ourselves when we feel as though we've failed or done something wrong. Imagine that your closest friend has gone through a similar situation. What would you say or do to help them feel better? Show yourself the same compassion.

Studies show that expressing gratitude improves relationships — and can be particularly beneficial if you have (or are) a partner who feels emotionally anxious or unsure. What do you appreciate most about your partner or loved ones? Find a way to show your gratitude to them today.

Create a community "kindness zone" — an area where people can drop off food or items they no longer need, and those that *do* need them can take them. Work with your local authority to do it, or try this in your street by organizing a "swap" day.

Bring all your senses into play when you look back on what you're grateful for today... which sight, sound, smell, taste and touch meant the most to you?

•••(14)•••

The words "I understand" can be so powerful, whether you're listening to a friend's problems, a colleague's work plan or an upset partner. Give them a try.

15

We must find time to stop and thank the people who make a difference in our lives.

JOHN F. KENNEDY

16

Judging other people's behaviour or life choices is, in some ways, a natural instinct, but it can be a negative habit as our judgements are often way off beam. Try to stop any such thoughts in their tracks today. Pause, remind yourself that we don't know other people's circumstances, and then give them the benefit of the doubt.

Be realistic in your expectations. If you set yourself impossible goals for the day, you're bound to end up feeling defeated at the end of it. Set a small manageable goal for yourself today — and celebrate when you achieve it.

Organize some family time-out with your nearest and dearest, whether it's a meal, a movie or a walk together. This is a kindness everyone will appreciate.

••• (19) •••

Be a support buddy: if you have a friend who's starting a fitness regime, for example, offer to share the journey with them and be there to give encouragement whenever they need it.

Does something in your town need a bit of TLC — a road sign that needs cleaning, a border that needs a trim or a bench that needs repainting? Get out there and do it — you're likely to meet a few appreciative people who might even give you a hand.

Find out if the organization you work for supports any charities. If not, is there a cause that they could sponsor? Talk to your colleagues and see if you can get something organized. Sponsoring a beehive is a good eco-option, or there may be a local hospice you could fundraise or provide materials for.

If you receive coupons that you won't use, leave them in the store for someone else to pick up, next to the relevant product. You can also forward any voucher codes you receive to friends who might use them.

Get creative with your recycling: did you know that crayons, toothbrushes and wine corks can be recycled, for example? Or how about cooking oil, engine oil, packing materials, razors, bicycles and training shoes? Do some research online and recycle something new this week.

•••(24)•••

Leave a note or card on someone's car wishing them a nice day.

••●(25)●••

We know it's polite to leave shared spaces clean and tidy after we've used them, but can you go one step further and prepare them for the next user? Could you adjust the car seat for your partner, or leave the shower at the right height for your housemate?

••●(26)●••

Treat people with kindness, because behind every face is a story that could use a little more love.

CHERYL RICHARDSON

Forgive someone for a past indiscretion — you'll be able to move forward with a lighter burden, and perhaps they will, too. This may mean building bridges in a friendship, or it may simply be that you forgive them in your thoughts — either way, it's a compassionate and positive step to take.

Forgive yourself. We often dwell on past events and blame ourselves for the way we acted (or didn't act), and we're usually being rather unfair to ourselves. Remember that you did the best you could in the circumstances, resolve to learn from your experience, and make an effort to move on.

29

Sometimes when we are generous in small, barely detectable ways it can change someone else's life forever.

MARGARET CHO

Sign up to a random acts of kindness group on social media and take inspiration from it every day. You could also try an app — such as BeKind — which will prompt you with ideas for kindnesses to carry out to keep the inspiration flowing.

july

01

Support local beekeepers (and bees!) by buying local, raw honey. Any effort to help our pollinators won't go to waste, and there are many health benefits to eating raw honey so you'll be doing yourself a kindness, too.

02

Can you put your specialist knowledge to good use on an online forum and advise others? Maybe you're a plumber, an expert knitter or brilliant at solving computer or phone glitches? It's satisfying to use your skills, and — of course — you'll be helping others at the same time.

Surprise a loved one with a special picnic. Pack up their favourite treats, drinks and a blanket, and head for the beach, countryside or forest to enjoy some time outdoors together. If the weather lets you down, take your picnic indoors instead.

Gratitude will shift you to a higher frequency, and you will attract much better things.

RHONDA BYRNE

••••(05)••••

Hold the elevator for someone or, if there's a queue, offer someone your place and take the stairs if you can. This is another considerate gesture that shows you're thinking of others during the daily rush.

Be kind to our forests by cutting down on paper waste and opting for paperless billing, using e-tickets for gigs and bookings, and not printing out emails or picking up superfluous leaflets.

••• 07 •••

If you use LinkedIn, leave an endorsement about a colleague's work. Alternatively, you could put a positive review on an industry website or offer to recommend someone who has done a good job for you.

••• 08 •••

New parents are often strapped for cash. Leaving a pack of baby supplies (nappies/diapers and wipes) at a changing station is a practical way to help.

Make a gratitude tree for your household — arrange some twigs in a jar and cut out some leaf shapes from cardboard. Have some string and a pen to hand so that your housemates can write the things they're grateful for onto the leaves and use them to decorate your tree.

Be kind to yourself by saying "no" to something you'd rather not do. If you're not in the mood to socialize, you could have a quiet night in, for example.

Check out gigs in your town or amateur productions of plays — buy tickets and go along to support local, new talent.

**Let's practise motivation and love,
not discrimination and hate.**

ZENDAYA

There will be times in our lives when we have to support our friends through difficult situations. Learning what to say at these moments will allow you to be as kind and tactful as possible. There's plenty of information online to help here, so do a little research into what to say to someone who is depressed, someone who has lost a loved one or who is facing ill health — you'll be able to offer the best kindness possible when they need it most.

The smallest act of kindness is worth more than the grandest intention.

ANONYMOUS

You can do yourself and the environment a kindness by buying a reusable water bottle and filling it up throughout the day. Dehydration affects our mood as well as our health, so you'll find yourself feeling brighter if you keep your fluid levels topped up.

••• 16 •••

Find yourself a penfriend — someone new to be kind to! — and enjoy swapping news and broadening your horizons. Receiving handwritten letters is always exciting.

••• •••

Most of these tips involve activities you can *do*. But have you ever thought about the kindness of *not* doing something? We've all got bad habits so, today, be brave and think about yours. Do you complain too much, or is your knuckle-cracking driving your flatmate mad? What can you give up as a kindness to others?

••• 18 •••

If there's a gloomy alley in your neighbourhood, or a row of garages that look a bit run-down, can you help to brighten them up? There's plenty of inspiration online for how to transform these areas with a splash of paint and – perhaps – the talents of young artists.

Be kind to yourself with a little reflexology. Massaging the centre of your palm will help to release anxiety, for example.

Love and kindness are never wasted. They always make a difference.

BARBARA DE ANGELIS

Let a colleague take the credit for something you've collaborated on, or sing their praises for their contribution, rather than taking the limelight for your part in the project.

Make a work colleague or housemate a hot drink when you make one for yourself. You can make it your undercover mission to notice what they like to drink! This is another example of how thoughtfulness will be appreciated just as much as the gesture itself.

How can you be a good sport? Have a think about what sportsmanship means to you and see if you can put these qualities into practice in everyday life. You could shake hands with a "competitor", support and encourage your "teammates" or know when to accept the judgement of the "ref" without arguing.

••• (**24**) •••

Celebrate other people's successes — whether it's a friend's house move or a colleague's promotion. Your interest and support will add to their joy and you'll experience more happiness yourself, too.

••• (**25**) •••

Look out for charity schemes that will reuse your old mobile phones or spectacles. When you're sending yours off, see if friends and family have any items to donate.

••• (**26**) •••

Scrawl it on the wall: random kindness and senseless acts of beauty.

ANNE HERBERT

In Japan, the tradition of *omotenashi* runs deep. It's all about anticipating the needs of others — particularly guests — and making discreet but effective gestures to help them feel valued. This is something we can all put into practice in some way — catering to a friend's dietary requirements, helping someone who's shy in company to feel comfortable or timing a get-together to suit someone else's commitments.

Take an interest in local developments and show up to consultation meetings to hear other people's point of view. It's important to take an active part in our communities and you may get the opportunity to contribute something.

Be kind to the planet by taking public transport, walking part of your journey, car-sharing or committing to a car-free weekend.

Do your little bit of good, where you are; it's those little bits of good put together that overwhelm the world.

DESMOND TUTU

Support a worthy cause by linking a charity to your Amazon account (go to www.smile.amazon.co.uk/com to select one).

august

Shopping for second-hand clothes (and other items) puts less demand on the planet's resources and – if you buy from a thrift store – you will be supporting a local charity, too.

Brighten up the pavement by buying some outdoor chalks and getting artistic, drawing smiley faces, flowers and anything that takes your fancy.

Make a scrapbook of a holiday or trip and gift it to whoever shared your adventure. Collect tickets, leaflets and – of course – take lots of photos to complete your project. Creative projects boost our mood and give us an end product to treasure.

• • • • • •

Can you practise the kindness of not giving up on someone? If a friend is avoiding your calls or unable to meet up, give them some space, but let them know you're there if they need you. Try not to take offence — they may be struggling with something and will be glad of your understanding when things return to normal.

• • • **05** • • •

There's evidence that experiencing the beauty of nature can lead to us behaving in a more generous way toward others. Make an effort to discover natural areas of beauty — you'll develop a kinder attitude to others, improve your own well-being and create some happy memories, too.

••• (06) •••

Learn some basic first-aid skills — or, even better, go on a training course — so that you're ready to help out if someone has a mishap.

••• (07) •••

Join a timebank (see www.timebanking.org in the UK and www.timebanks.org in the US) and exchange skills with others. You bank hours by carrying out tasks for other users, and then cash them in for help from others when you need it.

••• (08) •••

Regular exercise is a great way of putting yourself first — it will benefit you mentally and physically — and leave you feeling more relaxed and in a great place to be kind to others.

••● (09) ●••

The best way to cheer yourself up is to try to cheer somebody else up.

MARK TWAIN

••● (10) ●••

Go on a gratitude walk — walking is great therapy. Your only goal is to appreciate your surroundings as you go.

••● (11) ●••

Ask for donations of money for your birthday and spend your day carrying out an act of kindness for every year of your age. You could surprise strangers with flowers, for example. Take some photos of your efforts as a reminder of your day, and share to inspire others.

Studies have shown that performing several acts of kindness in one day can be even more beneficial than doing one kind thing a day. Consider setting aside some time once a week or fortnight to perform a series of compassionate acts. You could make Sunday evening your kindness session, for example, and carry out or plan kindnesses for the week ahead.

What can you do to look out for local wildlife? Searching online to find wildlife groups near you is a great start. There may be projects to support an endangered species, protect their habitat or to create a space for wildlife. Pick a cause and help out in any way you can.

When you're travelling on public transport, be thoughtful about where you sit, offering up seats with more legroom to family groups or people who may benefit from the extra space.

••• (15) •••

What could you do to help your colleagues enjoy some downtime together? Plan a game night, a regular sporting meet-up or a walk where anyone who wants to can turn up and chat along the way.

••• (16) •••

Try some baking... for pets! Handmade dog biscuits are fun to make. If you don't have or know a deserving dog, your local animal shelter may be grateful for your treats.

**Don't judge each day by
the harvest you reap but
by the seeds you plant.**

ROBERT LOUIS STEVENSON

Create a kindness space in your workplace or home. Put up positive postcards, quotes or pictures and invite others to add to it. People can take a card to brighten up their workspace or to give to someone they know who might need it. If you're creative you can add crocheted hearts or baked treats to your kindness corner.

Leave a pile of pennies by a fountain so passers-by can make a wish... or leave spare change at a parking machine to help out a stranger.

If you're visiting somewhere new, take home a souvenir for someone. A little token gift will show you're thinking of them, and giving presents is just as much fun as receiving them.

Get to know your neighbours: spend a little longer chatting to them, bake something to take round as a gift, or put a friendly note through their door introducing yourself or offering a helping hand if they need one.

••• (22) •••

Work on developing your patience — another valuable quality, and one that makes kindnesses much easier to carry out. Patience doesn't come easily to everyone, but like any skill it can be improved upon. The easiest way is to practise waiting for things — wait a few minutes longer before eating a treat, for example. (Studies have shown that we enjoy things more if we wait for them, too.)

••• (23) •••

Join your local climate action group — visit www.theclimategroup.org in the US and www.takeclimateaction.uk in the UK — and add your voice to the campaign to avert climate crisis. You'll stay informed on the latest petitions and demonstrations and be doing something practical to help the planet.

Be thankful for what you have; you'll end up having more.

OPRAH WINFREY

Write a poem for a friend — it could be funny or moving, it might describe something you've done together or sum up what your recipient means to you. There are no hard and fast rules with poetry — it doesn't have to rhyme. Anyone can write a poem, so have fun giving it a go.

••• 26 •••

Whether you're popping out for a coffee today, or going for a walk or a shopping trip, invite someone else along to enjoy the treat.

Let someone cut ahead of you in the queue at the shops if they're in a rush or only have a couple of items to buy.

Don't be the reason someone feels insecure. Be the reason someone feels seen, heard and supported.

CLEO WADE

••(29)•••

If you see a post on social media or an article in a magazine that a friend would like, pass it on. The words "I saw this and thought of you" will show you care.

If you have a little cash to spare, leave an extra generous tip for your server next time you eat out. Waiting tables is hard work and can feel like a thankless task, so your kindness will make a real difference.

Think about signing up for a course that could benefit yourself and others — horticultural skills, basic counselling, first-aid, DIY, meditation or life-coaching are all brilliant skills to have and to pass on. You may get really inspired and decide to make your new interest your career!

september

Could you help your local school? Most primary schools will be glad of volunteers to go in and listen to pupils learning to read. An hour a week can really make a difference, and it can be very rewarding. Alternatively, could you pass on a special skill or give an assembly about your vocation?

Put up a blackboard in your home and encourage your housemates to chalk up anything they're grateful for, along with positive messages or jokes to make each other smile. If you live alone, you can still create a gratitude board — and include motivational quotes about the power of kindness.

Treat everyone with politeness and kindness, not because they're nice, but because you are.

ROY T. BENNETT

••• (04) •••

Decorate pebbles with inspirational words — such as "Hope" or "Smile" — and give them to friends or leave in a public place to brighten a stranger's day.

••• (05) •••

This is a great time of year to build a bug hotel for insects to hibernate in. Simply bunch together some hollow stems or canes and hang them somewhere sheltered for bees to occupy over winter.

Create a book exchange box for your community. You could repurpose a phone booth or mailbox, club together to buy a purpose-made box or even make your own. Check out www.littlefreelibrary. org for inspiration.

••• 07 •••

We all find ourselves in situations that could turn into confrontations now and then, but if you learn how to stop an argument in its tracks you'll be doing everyone a kindness. Pause and taking a deep breath before you react to an opinion you disagree with, and then use one of these useful phrases: "You may be right", "I understand" or "I'll get back to you on that", and call time on the discussion.

Make your car more fuel-efficient by reducing your speed by around 10 km/hour (6 mph), removing excess weight from the boot and making sure your tyre pressure is correct.

The wonderful thing is that it's so incredibly easy to be kind.

INGRID NEWKIRK

Leave a bank note in the toy aisle to surprise a child and their parents. Add a note, inviting the finder to treat themselves to a toy. You'll make their day.

As the nights draw in, snuggle up with a classic book with kindness at its heart. *Little Women* is an excellent choice, as is *Charlotte's Web* or *The Boy at the Back of the Class*.

••• (12) •••

If an area in your life has changed — a friendship or a dynamic at work — reflect on whether you can adjust, too, and take a more compassionate stance in the new status quo.

••• (13) •••

A simple kindness for butterflies is to leave an overripe banana out for them to feed on, to supplement the lower levels of nectar around at this time of year.

••●(14)●••

Who was the teacher who influenced you most? Whether it was someone who believed in your abilities, inspired you to pursue your favourite subject or was simply great at their job, consider writing them a note to tell them how much they meant to you, and what you've ended up doing. Teachers invest so much time in their students but don't often get to see the results of their hard work, so your letter will mean a lot.

••●(15)●••

There is no duty more indispensable than that of returning a kindness.

MARCUS TULLIUS CICERO

••• (16) •••

Consider giving someone the gift of an experience rather than a physical present. You might choose cinema tickets, a manicure or passes to a gig — whatever you think your recipient will enjoy.

••• (17) •••

Using your workmates' names when you speak to them can create a much friendlier atmosphere. (Don't go over the top, though!)

••• (18) •••

Relive a special memory for someone who'll appreciate it — either by digging out photos and talking about the memories they bring up, or even by recreating an old photo or a celebration.

Take a look at your body language today. Would you like to appear more open or approachable? You may be able to work on the way you sit or stand, or your expression when speaking to others.

I believe that one person can make a difference.

GRETA THUNBERG

Put some extra care into preparing a foodie treat. It will make whoever you're cooking for feel loved — even if it's just for you!

Friends are a great source of joy in our lives, but it's easy to neglect friendships when we get bogged down with work or other commitments. Invite a friend round for a catch-up or send them a card to make them smile.

• • • (23) • • •

It's all too easy to take people who work in our community for granted – the refuse collectors and mail delivery personnel, the bus drivers and the people who maintain parks and communal spaces. Find a way to show your appreciation to someone today – stopping to say hello and thank you is a great start.

••• •••

What can you do to bring people together? If you have friends who have lost touch, could you organize a reunion or get-together to renew those connections?

••• (25) •••

Be a peacemaker. If you have friends who have fallen out, perhaps you could help to smooth things over.

••• (26) •••

Send someone a bunch of flowers — or have chocolates delivered to them. Nothing beats the excitement of receiving an unexpected special delivery. Flowers aren't cheap, but you could get together with a friend to organize this surprise.

••• (27) •••

Kindness in words creates confidence. Kindness in thinking creates profoundness. Kindness in giving creates love.

LAO TZU

Adjusting your diet can be a way of being kind to the planet and kind to yourself. Research shows that cutting down on meat will drastically reduce your carbon footprint — and there are health benefits to be had, too. Perhaps you could have a vegetarian or vegan day every week. Give some thought to where and how your food is sourced and try to pick options that are kindest to the planet and our fellow creatures.

••• 29 •••

This week, think about recognizing the achievements of someone who has gone unnoticed. This could either be through researching an unsung historical figure online — a humanitarian or pioneer -- or by sharing the story of a local hero and ensuring they get the recognition they deserve.

••• 30 •••

If you find yourself speaking rapidly, talking over others or issuing quick-fire instructions at work, make an effort to slow... it... down! Slowing the pace will make communications more comfortable, and bring a feeling of calm to the day for everyone.

october

Get baking and share your creations with your work colleagues or housemates. If cakes aren't your thing, you could try making jams, pickles, toffee or bread. Homecooked treats are always appreciated, and cooking can be a very soothing activity, too.

Leave a legacy of kindness by planting a tree. You'll not only be adding something beautiful to your backyard or garden, you'll also be providing wildlife with a habitat, encouraging birds and insects to visit. Do a little online research or visit a garden centre for advice on what will suit your climate and budget — then get digging!

If you don't have space to plant a tree at home, consider sponsoring a tree or dedicating a tree to a loved one. Check out www.nationalforest.org for ideas.

Buy up a few pairs of warm socks and keep them in your car or bag to give out next time you see someone sleeping outside.

For beautiful lips, speak only words of kindness.

AUDREY HEPBURN

Host a kindness evening: get together a group of friends, invite everyone to share a story of how a compassionate act has changed someone's life and see if you can come up with ideas for kindnesses you can carry out as a group for your community.

If your kindness get-together is a success, why not form a kindness club? You could meet up regularly, sharing positivity, inspiration and ideas. Your get-togethers will be a source of happiness for everyone involved and will also give you the opportunity to show kindness to one another, of course.

••• (08) •••

Leave sticky notes with positive messages in public places to cheer up passers-by. "You're awesome" is a good start! (Alternatively, you could draw a smiley face or write a joke for them to enjoy.) You could leave these around your home or workplace, too.

••• (09) •••

Leave credit in a vending machine for the next user.

••• (10) •••

Don't forget to take a little time out for your daily gratitude practice. When you wake up today, spend a few moments feeling grateful for the day ahead and identify — or plan — something to be extra thankful for.

If someone you know has always wanted to go to a particular restaurant or visit somewhere nearby, organize a trip and to do it together. If that someone is you, well, you deserve a treat, too — book tickets or schedule time this week to make it happen.

Consider filling a shoe box for someone in need this Christmas. There are lots of charities that organize these wonderful schemes, so search online for details. If your box is destined for children abroad, you'll need to get it ready ahead of time. (There are schemes that allow you to put together a box for people in care homes, too.)

Can you give your support to a new vlogger, blogger or YouTuber who is just starting out? Search for someone who is creating good quality content that interests you, subscribe to their channel and share their posts.

If you're a keen crafter, could you put together starter kits to encourage friends to try out your hobby? You could give these as gifts to people or even offer them a tutorial to get them started, if it's something tricky. It's a great way of passing on your skills and ensuring that you both take some time out to relax.

●●● (15) ●●●

Let gratitude be the pillow upon which you kneel to say your nightly prayer.

MAYA ANGELOU

●●● (16) ●●●

How can you show solidarity for someone? Solidarity goes one step further than empathizing — it means taking action and lightening their load. If a friend is grieving, can you sit with them and share their grief? Can you forgo something that someone else has no choice in missing out on? Or could you make a gesture to someone in your community who is suffering, to show your support?

••• (17) •••

Offer hope — if someone is in a difficult situation, try to find a ray of hope for them to focus on. Be sure to validate their feelings and concerns, but offering some light at the end of the tunnel can be a great comfort.

••• (18) •••

Carry out a random act of kindness with a friend; it will benefit everyone involved and build a great bond with your pal, too.

••• (19) •••

Treat someone to their favourite chocolate bar or snack. Slip it into their bag for a surprise later in the day.

Make up a care kit for someone in your community who is currently homeless. You could include a toothbrush and paste, wet wipes, socks, gloves, hat, protein bars or snacks. Aim for something small and portable but practical. Be safe and sincere when you hand out your kit(s).

If someone comes to speak to you, show them that they have your attention by closing your laptop or putting down your phone and turning toward them. It's polite — of course! — but will also make for a more positive interaction.

••• (**22**) •••

Feed someone else's parking meter or hand over a parking ticket which hasn't elapsed for a fellow driver to use.

••• (**23**) •••

It's a fun idea to learn a few party games so you can break the ice if you're with people who don't know one another well. If you're really brave, you can try them out the next time your train is delayed!

••• (**24**) •••

How are you getting on with your energy-saving activities (see 27 April, page 56)? Check your progress and see how you can improve things further – can you switch to energy-saving lightbulbs or turn down the thermostat in your home?

25

You cannot do a kindness too soon, for you never know how soon it will be too late.

RALPH WALDO EMERSON

Tap in to the benefits of "breathing breaks" — moments during the day when you pause and focus on breathing deeply, right down into your diaphragm. This will boost your mental and physical health and leave you feeling calmer (and ready to be kind!). Spread the word among your friends and colleagues about this simple tip and they can enjoy the benefits, too.

•••● 27 ●•••

If you're having a sort out, check online as some items you wouldn't expect can be donated to charity — lightly used make-up or toiletries are welcomed by some women's refuges, for example.

•••● 28 ●•••

One of the best ways to benefit your local area is to provide a bench at a beauty spot or anywhere it will be useful. If you can't fund this yourself, perhaps you can get together with neighbours to do so... or find someone practical to make it.

•••● 29 ●•••

Share the gift of laughter with a friend and sit down to watch an episode of your favourite comedy show together.

If you know someone who is hurt or angry, think about the best way to help them vent their feelings — whether that's hosting a plate-smashing party or offering a sympathetic ear. Your goal is to assist them in offloading those emotions so they can move on.

A group craft project for someone special is rewarding for everyone involved. You could get your friends to knit a square each and sew them together to make a rug or quilt together — the experienced knitters can show the newbies what to do — or get everyone to sign a tablecloth and embroider the signatures. A scrapbook with messages or pictures from everyone is a good option, too.

november

If you or someone close to you has lost a loved one, remembering them is a way of showing gratitude for all they mean to you. If it is a friend who has lost someone special, remembering the anniversary of their loss is important, helping to ensure that people don't feel alone during times of sadness or difficulty.

Compassion isn't about solutions. It's about giving all the love that you've got.

CHERYL STRAYED

Take a look at the www.globalgiving.com website for ideas of different projects you and your friends could support overseas. The projects have all been vetted by the organization, and you can explore them by country or type (wildlife protection, clean water or mental health, for example). There's plenty of information about each project, including case studies and photos.

Host a pamper evening with friends or just for you. It can be as simple as buying some skincare masks and a bottle of wine, or you could really go to town with the pampering products and treat yourself to a home spa.

••• (05) •••

Take a stand against domestic violence by donating, if you can, to a charity such as Refuge, which can supply care packages for an individual escaping from domestic abuse. In the US visit www.futureswithoutviolence.org to see what you can do to help.

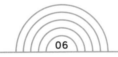

06

What wisdom can you find that is greater than kindness?

JEAN-JACQUES ROUSSEAU

••• (07) •••

See if any of the everyday items you throw away could be collected for charity — milk bottle tops and postage stamps are good examples.

Write out some "kindness coupons" and give them to your nearest and dearest to trade in for a hug, a day off from the washing-up or a promise to cook dinner, for example.

Treat your household to some *hygge* to brighten up winter evenings – get out some warm blankets and hot chocolate, light some candles and snuggle up to watch a favourite TV show.

•••（10）•••

Good manners show courtesy to those around us. As well as saying "please" and "thank you" think about other ways to show consideration, such as by being punctual, and not criticizing others or being boastful.

How could you provide a meal for someone in need? Could you buy takeaway food for someone struggling with homelessness or help out at a meal centre? Making a meal for a neighbour who lives alone, works long hours or doesn't have time to prepare food is another option that will be much appreciated.

Studies have shown that hugging reduces stress and boosts the immune system, heart health and happiness. Even better: one hug benefits two people, which is a bargain! So hug someone today — if hugging is not your style, a simple touch on the arm is effective, too.

Celebrate World Kindness Day in your home or workplace by challenging everyone to come up with an act of kindness to carry out. You could even get together in a group and hand out sweets or treats in your local town.

The more grateful I am, the more beauty I see.

MARY DAVIS

••• (15) •••

Think about whether you have more than you need of something — household supplies, food or free time — and find someone to share it with. Focusing on what we can give, rather than what we have, is at the root of all kindness.

••● ●••

It's time for a self-kindness check-in. Think about your daily routine and ensure you're getting enough sleep, eating properly and looking after your body by doing exercise that brings you joy.

••● 17 ●••

Trust and kindness are closely linked. Saying "I trust you" is a powerful way to boost the confidence of someone who's unsure about their capabilities. See if you can encourage someone by showing your trust in them today.

••● 18 ●••

Take a look at the green credentials of your energy provider and see if you can switch to one that uses renewable sources of energy.

19

Choose love, give love.
Love everyone, always.

HARRY STYLES

Be kind to birds by putting out a dish of fresh water plus a feeder with nuts and seeds to provide them with a dependable source of food in the colder months. You could repurpose a plastic bottle to make your feeder and earn eco points at the same time. Other treats your garden visitors will enjoy include tinned dog or cat food, cooked rice and cheese.

Clean a communal area at work — such as the kitchen — or add a vase of flowers to a corner to brighten it up for everybody.

・・●(22)●・・

When you think about the achievement you're most proud of, it's a nice idea to consider the support you received along the way to help you reach your goal. Take a moment today to acknowledge everyone's contribution and send them grateful thoughts.

・・●(23)●・・

Contribute to a giving day, such as #GivingTuesday, where people rally round to support a 24-hour online fundraising challenge for a particular cause. (See www.givingtuesday.org.uk for more information.)

In Sweden there is a tradition that eating *pepparkakor* (delicious, thin gingerbread cookies) will make you kind. They are a popular choice for *fika* — a break shared with friends or work colleagues, where everyone stops what they're doing for a daily coffee and a chat together. So why not start a *fika* tradition in your workplace or home? There are lots of recipes online for baking *pepparkakor*, which smell wonderful, or if you don't have time to bake, they're easily bought in supermarkets or a certain Swedish furniture store!

You can always, always give something, even if it is only kindness!

ANNE FRANK

••• •••

Talking about kindness helps others to recognize its importance and change their focus, too. It's easy to introduce stories of kindness into a conversation, so give it a try today.

••• (27) •••

Collect all those spare coins that clog up your purse or pocket and donate them to charity.

••• (28) •••

Practise tuning in to your intuition and acting from a place of kindness without worrying about what other people may think of you. Concern about what people may think of us can be an obstacle to kind behaviour, but you can overcome it with practice!

••• (29) •••

Educate yourself a little about anxiety and depression, along with a few good tips on how to cope with it and who to call when things get tough. You'll be in a strong position to advise your friends if they struggle with these issues.

••• (30) •••

Buddhist monk Ajahn Brahm coined the term "kindfulness" to combine the concepts of being kind and mindful toward others. One way to share this attitude with others is to create a kindfulness space at home or work – find a calm uncluttered corner, remove any distractions, and add somewhere to sit comfortably, some plants and natural imagery and some soothing sounds.

december

01

If you have children, nieces or nephews, teach them the power of compassion by inviting them to carry out random acts of kindness with you — you'll be creating kindness activists of the future. For older children, pick topics that interest them — such as activism or volunteering in a particular area.

02

If you truly pour your heart into what you believe in, even if it makes you vulnerable, amazing things can and will happen.

EMMA WATSON

••• (03) •••

Search for Christmas volunteering opportunities near you — helping at a foodbank, soup kitchen or homeless centre, delivering meals or gifts. Of course, any of these places will also gratefully receive donations if you don't have the time to help out in person.

••• (04) •••

Giving blood is an amazing act of kindness that can save someone's life. To find out more about the process visit www.blood.co.uk or www.americasblood.org.

••• (05) •••

It's easy to help those we know and get on with, but today see if you can seek out someone that you're not on such good terms with and help them, too.

Try your hand at making jam, soap or handmade beauty products, such as lip balms or facial scrubs, to give as gifts. You can repurpose jars or other containers to package your makes and add a pretty label and ribbon.

Perhaps you will forget tomorrow the kind words you say today, but the recipient may cherish them over a lifetime.

DALE CARNEGIE

Creating a "ripple stone" is a lovely idea that gives you the chance to get your craft materials out. Decorate a stone and add the words "Passing on the kindness." Then do a good deed for a friend and hand them the stone so that they can pay it forward, too.

●●● (09) ●●●

Can you campaign for kindness to become part of your company or organization's mission statement — a value that they will promote? Often kindness can be overlooked in the workplace as it's not something that can be easily measured, but there are plenty of examples of how kindness at work benefits everyone.

The Salvation Army make it easy for you to buy a gift for a child who wouldn't otherwise receive one, via the Christmas Present appeal (in the UK) and the Angel Tree programme (in the US) — so consider giving a gift to one of these causes this year.

An important part of gratitude practice is remembering the bad times — when you remind yourself of how difficult things have been, it provides a stark contrast for the blessings you have around you today, and you can appreciate them more.

Treat someone to a surprise meal by ordering their favourite food to be delivered.

13

We rise by lifting others.

ROBERT INGERSOLL

If you're planning to give people presents at Christmas, consider charity donations that will be meaningful for your recipient — such as sponsoring an animal or planting a tree — rather than buying items that may be unwanted and end up going to waste. The charity will benefit, and both you and your recipient will get the satisfaction of knowing that you've made a difference this holiday season.

If you're unsure how to act in any situation, don't overcomplicate things. "If you don't know what to do, just be kind" is a great mantra, and well worth displaying somewhere prominent!

16

Look for easy ways to support charity without even thinking about it — such as signing up for a payroll giving scheme if your employer offers one, choosing to donate any tax rebates to charity, or by ticking the Gift Aid box if you're a UK taxpayer.

17

Buy Fairtrade (Fair Trade Certified, in the US) goods when you can — you'll be helping to support people in developing countries.

At times, our own light goes out and is rekindled by a spark from another person.

ALBERT SCHWEITZER

••• (19) •••

Indulge in some inspiration by watching a feel-good series that has a strong moral compass, with kindness and compassion at its heart. Vintage shows and period dramas can be great for this — think *Downton Abbey*, *Call the Midwife* or *The Brady Bunch*.

••• (20) •••

Remember to show interest in others by asking for people's opinions when you chat. It's a great courtesy to give other people the chance to express themselves and to have their point of view acknowledged.

21

You know that outstanding chore that's been bugging everyone, such as changing the lightbulb in the hallway or putting out the trash? Be the person who takes action and gets the job done.

22

Reach out to someone in your community who is alone and may find the festive season a difficult time. You could take a small gift round to a neighbour and stay for a chat or invite someone in for a coffee, for example.

23

Show consideration for others who may not celebrate the holiday season for personal or religious reasons, and who find this time of year difficult.

●●● (24) ●●●

Consider your close relationships and whether you're putting too much pressure on others to behave in a certain way or to work toward a goal they may not share.

●●● (25) ●●●

Imagine a day where you wake up full of excitement at the chance to show your loved ones how much they mean to you, a day full of gifts... And remember, you can experience that 365 times a year.

●●● (26) ●●●

Sending a thank-you to someone who has given you a gift could really make their day — a written thank-you note is lovely, but a text saying what you love about your present will mean a lot, too.

27

Kindness is always fashionable, and always welcome.

AMELIA BARR

••• 28 •••

Organizing a light-hearted end-of-year awards ceremony for your family, friendship group or workmates is enormous fun. You can make the awards as silly as you like: "Most likely to go to jail", "Most embarrassing moment", and so on. You can get creative with prizes — duct tape for the best problem solver; a rock for the "You rock" award. Don't forget to include some heartfelt compliments as you hand out the awards, too.

If someone shares their plans with you, be supportive of their ambitions and ideas — don't be sceptical. Enthusiasm is a wonderful quality to cultivate and share.

••• (30) •••

Read through your journal and reflect on your year of kindness. Think about the difference you've made to other people's lives — could you write a blog entry or social media post about your experience to inspire other people to do the same?

••• (31) •••

Look back on your year with gratitude for everything you're received and achieved... and look forward to another year filled with kindness ahead.

conclusion

Now that you and your loved ones have enjoyed the benefits of a year packed full of kindness, you'll have seen how easy it can be to brighten someone's day with even the smallest of gestures. Hopefully you've also experienced a lot to be grateful for yourself, and practised plenty of self-compassion, too.

Although you've reached the end of the book, your kindness journey is, of course, far from over. After all, there's a whole new year ahead just waiting for you to transform it — one act of kindness at a time.

notes

....

....

....

....

....

....

....

....

....

....

....

....

Have you enjoyed this book?
If so, find us on Facebook at
Summersdale Publishers, on Twitter
at @Summersdale and on Instagram
at @summersdalebooks and get in
touch. We'd love to hear from you!

www.summersdale.com